Why We Left

I Remember
PALESTINE

Anita Ganeri

RAINTREE
STECK-VAUGHN
PUBLISHERS
The Steck-Vaughn Company

Austin, Texas

Published by Raintree Steck-Vaughn Publishers, an imprint of Steck-Vaughn Company

Editors: Sally Matthews, Jim Pipe, Edith Vann
Designer: Tessa Barwick
Cover Design: Joyce Spicer
Illustrator: David Burroughs
Photo Research: Brooks Krikler Research

Library of Congress Cataloging-in-Publication Data

Ganeri, Anita, 1961–
    I remember Palestine / Anita Ganeri.
      p. cm. — (Why we left)
    Includes index.
    ISBN 0-8114-5610-2
    1. Palestinian Arabs — Juvenile literature. 2. Palestine — Juvenile literature. 3. Israel — Juvenile literature. 4. Jewish-Arab relations — Juvenile literature. [1. Palestinian Arabs. 2. Palestine. 3. Israel.] I. Title. II. Series.
DS113.6.G36 1995
956.94–dc20   94-21853
                  CIP AC

Printed and bound in Belgium

1 2 3 4 5 6 7 8 9 0 PR 99 98 97 96 95 94

CONTENTS

Introduction

My name is Ahmad, and I am Palestinian. Palestine is not a country. You won't see its name on most maps. Palestine is the historical name of a region between the Mediterranean Sea and the Jordan River. A country called Israel is now in this area. This land is the home of the Palestinian Arabs and the Israeli Jews. My family and I left Israel because of the terrible fighting between these two groups. They are both struggling over the same piece of land.

I'd like to tell you about my old home, not just about its troubles. I'll also tell you about the people, the country, and our way of life.

There are over 4.5 million Palestinians in the world. About 2 million live in Israel and the Israeli Occupied Territories of Gaza and the West Bank. Another 2.5 million live in other countries. Many live in neighboring Arab countries. Others live in North Africa. Some live farther away in the United States and other Western countries. Today there are 2 million Palestinian refugees listed by the United Nations.

Country and Climate

Israel (Palestine) covers a very small area. It is only about the size of the state of New Jersey. It is located on the eastern shore of the Mediterranean Sea. Its neighbors are Lebanon and Syria to the north, Jordan to the east, and Egypt to the south. The Gaza Strip is in the southwest. The West Bank lies along one side of the Jordan River, in the east (right). The geography is very different, depending on which part of the country you're in. Mountains, green valleys, hot deserts, rivers, and lakes may all be found in Israel (Palestine). The Jordan River is the country's longest. It flows through the Sea of Galilee in the north to the Dead Sea in the south. The Dead Sea is the lowest point on the Earth's surface. This sea gets its name because its water is far too salty for anything to live in it.

The climate varies from one part of the country to the next. Summers are hot and dry. Winters are cool and mild. This type of climate is called a "temperate" climate. Almost all the rain falls in the winter, between November and March. In the hilly areas there is even some snow. It is much hotter in the desert. Daytime temperatures reach 104°F (40°C). At night, though, the desert is freezing cold.

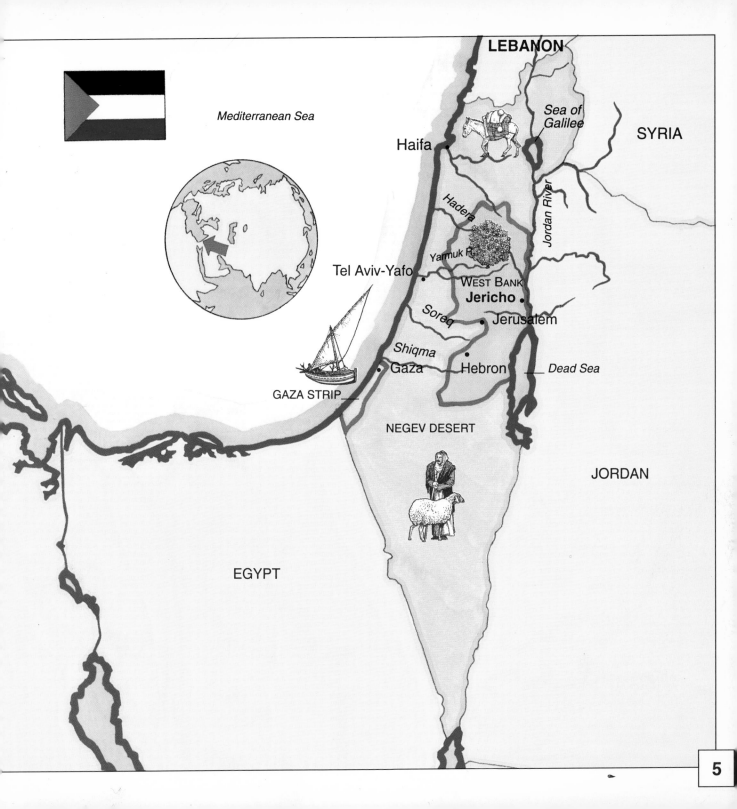

LEBANON

Mediterranean Sea

SYRIA

Haifa

Sea of Galilee

Hadeia

Jordan River

Yarmuk R.

Tel Aviv-Yafo

WEST BANK
Jericho

Soreq

Jerusalem

Shiqma

Gaza

Hebron

Dead Sea

GAZA STRIP

NEGEV DESERT

JORDAN

EGYPT

5

History of an Ancient Land

The land we call Palestine has a long and important past. Its early history is recorded in the Bible.

About 1900 B.C., the Hebrews, ancestors of the Jews, settled in the area. By 1000 B.C., the Hebrews set up the kingdom of Israel, ruled by King David. The Jews believe that Palestine is the land promised to them by God. In return they had to obey His commandments. Later Ancient Israel divided into two countries before Palestine was taken over by the Babylonians, Greeks, and Romans, among others. The Romans drove most Jews away from Palestine in 70 A.D. and 135 A.D. to punish the Jews for two revolts against Roman rule. The Jews became refugees as they settled all over the world.

Palestine is the historical land where most of the events in the Bible took place. For example, Jesus was born in Bethlehem, a town now in the West Bank. Jesus was baptized by John the Baptist (left) on the west bank of the Jordan River.

The Promised Land

The Arabs took control of Palestine and much of the Middle East from the Romans in the seventh century A.D. The area was first ruled by the Muslims. Today's Palestinians are the ancestors of these early Arabs. Over time the original Islamic Arabs were replaced by other Muslims who were not solely Arab. These people were the Abbasids, the Mamluks, and finally, the Ottoman Turks.

For hundreds of years after the Romans forced the Jews out of Palestine, the Jews were treated very badly in the various lands in which they lived. They never forgot their dream of returning to Palestine. The killing of millions of Jews by the Nazis during World War II (1939-45) caused thousands of Jews to leave Europe. Many of them went to Palestine. This desperate situation in Europe made the founding of a Jewish state even more important.

Jews believe that over 3,000 years ago, Moses led their people back to the "promised land." They followed him from Egypt (right).

A Divided Nation

In 1947, the United Nations decided to divide Palestine into one Arab and one Jewish country. On May 15, 1948, the new State of Israel was declared. War immediately broke out with the Arabs, who refused to accept a Jewish state in Palestine. Israel won this war with the Arabs, so the Jewish state remained. Many Palestinian Arabs left during the 1948 war because of the fighting. They became refugees and were not allowed to return home after the war. Not all Palestinian Arabs left during the fighting, however. Some stayed and became part of the new Jewish state of Israel.

In 1967, Israel captured Gaza and the West Bank from its Arab neighbors in another war. Since then, these areas have been called the Occupied Territories. Most countries do not believe that Israel had a right to add them to its territory. Although some Jews tried to settle in the Occupied Territories after 1967, most of the people who live there are Palestinian Arabs.

The Palestinian People

The Palestinians became very bitter after 1948. They felt that the Jewish dream came true at the price of the Palestinian Arabs. Today we Palestinians still have no country of our own. But there are Palestinian people living all over the world. There are still many Palestinians living in Israel or in the Occupied Territories. Most Palestinians, however, live outside Palestine. Many live in the neighboring Arab countries of Jordan, Lebanon, and Syria. Others live farther away in North Africa, the Persian Gulf countries, and even the United States.

Many Palestinians are very poor and live in refugee camps or slums. However, there are also many successful Palestinians who have good jobs and live well. Palestinians living outside Israel are known for their skills and high level of education. There is a higher percentage of Palestinians who are university graduates than many other national groups. Their skills have been important to the growth of many of the countries in which they live. The pictures on the right show Palestinian people, both young and old.

Much of the land is dry desert. Water is scarce. However, over the last 30 years the Israelis have taken on large irrigation projects. Water is now pumped and piped from the rivers and lakes in the north of the country to turn the dry and dusty lands in the south into growing green fields. The amount of water needed by the Israeli farmers for this is enormous. Palestinian farmers complain that little water is left for them to use on their small farms. The struggle over water has become a major part of the problem between Israelis and Palestinians.

Rural Life

Many Palestinians are poor farmers, living in small villages in the Occupied Territories. They grow crops such as lemons, oranges (left), olives, grapes, lentils, beans, and chick-peas on small, private farms. Some farmers also raise goats, sheep, and chickens.

Some Palestinian farmers are angry because the Israeli government has taken their land. The Palestinians are also upset by Israeli settlers who have started their own farms in the Occupied Territories on what was once Palestinian land. Many Palestinians now work on Israeli farms, instead of farming their own land.

Some of the Israeli farms are large group ones called kibbutzim. Many Jewish families live and work together on these large farms. Everyone owns the land and harvests it as a group.

Olive trees (right) have been grown in the area since the time of the Bible.

City Life

Since ancient times, Jerusalem has been the capital of Palestine. During the 1948 war, the city of Jerusalem was divided between the Arabs and Jews. The new state of Israel declared Jerusalem its capital, even though it only controlled the western part of the city. In the 1967 war, the Israelis captured the eastern half of the city. Though the city was officially joined together in 1967, two parts remain. West Jerusalem has more modern buildings. Most of the people there are Jewish. East Jerusalem (left) is much older and has an ancient wall around it. It is the Arab half of the city.

Many Palestinians go to the cities in search of work. As a result, the cities in the Occupied Territories are becoming crowded. Since the West Bank and Gaza are occupied territories, Israeli soldiers, barbed wire, and other signs of rule by the army are common sights.

Arab markets are called *souqs*. There you can buy fresh fruit and vegetables, nuts, spices, leather, and sandals. You can also watch people at work, making beautiful objects of brass and silver.

Life in the Camps

In 1948, the State of Israel was formed. Because of the fighting that broke out between Arabs and Jews, many Palestinian Arabs were forced to leave their homes. They became refugees, living in camps in the Occupied Territories and in neighboring countries, such as Lebanon and Jordan. In 1950, the U.N. set up the UNRWA (United Nations Relief Works Agency) for Palestinian refugees. This group helps refugees with food, health, and schooling.

More than 40 years later, many Palestinians still live in these poor refugee camps. Although the camps were not supposed to last for long when they were first built, the struggle between Palestinians and Israelis has lasted much longer than expected. Many Palestinians have been born and brought up in the camps, like me. They have never known any other life. Most of the older people came to the camps with only their memories of their old homes and their dreams of returning to Palestine one day.

Life in the refugee camps is very hard. There are simple huts and unpaved alleys (right). Many of the camps are overcrowded. This situation is made worse by the increasing number of Palestinians. Some of the camps in the Gaza Strip have over 40,000 people living in them.

Food and Clothes

We eat such food as pita bread, falafel (deep-fried chick-pea balls), hummus (chick-pea paste), lamb, and chicken dishes served with rice, nuts, and vegetables such as eggplant. For candy we eat halvah (sesame seed nougat). The picture (bottom right) shows an ordinary Palestinian meal. Neither Muslims nor Jews are allowed to eat pork. Muslims are not allowed to drink alcohol. But strong black Turkish coffee is a very well-liked drink.

Our clothes are long, loose robes and headdresses. They keep us cool and protect us from the hot sun and desert dust. Many people now wear Western-style clothes. But these are not as well suited to the weather as our Arab clothes. Muslim women must cover their bodies. So our style of dress is designed to do this, too.

Palestinian men wear a headdress called a *kafiyya*. It is a large, square scarf wrapped around the head. It is held in place with a twisted band called an *ogaal*.

Falafel is sold at stands by the road (left), rather than hamburgers (above). Falafel is the Palestinians' favorite fast food. It is probably one of the oldest types of fast foods in the world.

Customs

Palestinians follow their own Arabic customs and ways of doing things. These are often linked with the rules of Islam.

Our families often arrange for us to be married. There is a simple wedding, followed by a great feast. Family and friends bring presents and join in the feast and celebration (right). Family life is very important to Arabs. Often our whole families, including our grandparents, uncles, aunts, and cousins, all live near each other.

As children we are taught good manners. We also learn to respect our parents, teachers, and neighbors.

In our spare time, we like to play soccer and other games. We perform Arabic dancing for special events. We listen to poetry and music. These men are playing a very popular game called backgammon. They are smoking a water pipe, called a *narghila*, and drinking Turkish coffee.

Beliefs

Palestine is a special place for Jews, Christians, and Muslims alike. Most Palestinian Arabs are Muslims, as I am. We follow the religion of Islam. We believe there is only one God, called Allah, and His last and greatest prophet was Muhammad. Our holy book, the Quran, contains rules on how we should live.

Some Palestinian Arabs are Christians. They believe in the teachings of Jesus, who lived in Palestine 2,000 years ago. The story of his life is recorded in the Bible.

Most Israelis are Jews. Their holiest book is the Torah. It contains God's commandments to Moses. Both Judaism and Christianity first began in Palestine.

Muslims pray five times a day. We kneel down and pray in the direction of Mecca. Often we pray in mosques, but we are allowed to pray in any clean place whether inside or outside.

Jerusalem is full of holy places. The Wailing Wall (above) is the holiest place for the Jews. It was part of an ancient Jewish building. The Dome of the Rock (left) is special to Muslims. We believe that this is where Muhammad began a night journey to heaven. The Church of the Nativity (below) is thought to be the place where Jesus was born. It is located in the small town of Bethlehem in the West Bank.

Palestinians (above) demonstrate for the right to rule themselves in the Occupied Territories, free from the daily restrictions imposed by Israeli soldiers, barricades, and barbed wire fences (top and bottom right).

Politics

The fight between Jews and Arabs, which has lasted more than 70 years, lies at the center of our political life. Although Palestinians who live in Israel itself are citizens and can take part in Israeli elections, Palestinians who live in the Occupied Territories cannot. Life under rule by the army is always very difficult. Israeli soldiers have the right to arrest people without asking why. They can also hold prisoners without trial.

In 1964, the Palestinian Liberation Organization (PLO) was set up to represent us. The PLO has been led by Yasir Arafat (right) since 1968. For many years, the PLO and Israelis fought. Some groups in the PLO hijacked airplanes and killed innocent people. The Israelis then attacked innocent Palestinian refugees in Lebanon. With so much killing on both sides, peace talks have been difficult.

In December 1987, the Palestinians living in the Occupied Territories began fighting against Israeli rule. This movement was called the *intifada*, or uprising. What we want is to rule ourselves in the West Bank and Gaza. In 1988, the PLO accepted that the struggle with Israel could not be solved with killing. Lately peace talks between the Israelis and the PLO have improved.

The Future

In September 1993, the leader of the PLO, Yasir Arafat, and the
Israeli prime minister, Yitzhak Rabin, signed the first stage of a peace
agreement in Washington, D.C. (left). They agreed that the
Israelis would begin to pull out of the Occupied
Territories. They also agreed to talk more about
Palestinian self-rule. On May 18, 1994, the Gaza Strip
and the town of Jericho began Palestinian self-rule.
There are still many problems to be solved. We don't
know what will happen to all of the Palestinian
refugees who live outside of Israel and the Occupied
Territories. We also don't know what the final
shape of Palestinian rule will be in the West Bank
and Gaza. There are also many Israelis and
Palestinians who are against peace.

Like millions of other Palestinians, my family
would love to return to our country. But I don't
know if this will ever happen. There is much
hatred and lack of trust on both sides.

Perhaps peace is not far off, and we will have
our own place to live in as we choose. Maybe
then I can return to Palestine and see my
friends and relatives.

Fact File

Land and People

Name: Palestine (a historical land, not a country)

Location: On eastern end of Mediterranean Sea

Main languages: Arabic, Hebrew

Population: 4,748,000 (of Israel now)

Landmarks

Major river: Jordan

Major Sea: Dead Sea, 1,312 feet below sea level (-400 m), the lowest point on the land surface of the Earth

Weather

Climate: Temperate, with hot, dry summers and cool, mild winters

Cities

Important cities and towns: Jerusalem, Jericho, Bethlehem

Trade and Industry

Mineral resources: Sulphur, potash, phosphate, manganese, copper

Culture

Ethnic groups: 15% Arab, 85% Jewish

Main religions: Islam, Jewish (Palestine is a holy place for Muslims, Jews, and Christians.)

Literacy rate: 92%, Jewish; 70%, Arab

Food and Farming

Major Crops: Lemons, oranges, olives, grapes, lentils, beans, chick-peas

Livestock: Goats, sheep, chickens

Government

Treaty: PLO-Israeli peace treaty signed in Washington in the fall of 1993, for Israeli withdrawal from the Occupied Territories

Limited self-rule: May 18, 1994, Gaza Strip and West Bank town of Jericho under Palestinian self-rule

Occupied Territories: West Bank and the Gaza Strip

Intifada: Palestinians in the Occupied Territories march against Israeli rule in a movement in 1987 called the *intifada*, or uprising

Index

Photographic Credits:

Front cover, pp. 4, 6, 11, 12-13 (all), 14 (bottom left and right), 21 (top left), 24-25 (all), 26 (all): Eye Ubiquitous; Title page: Spectrum Colour Library; Front cover inset, pp. 3, 21 (bottom), 29: Roger Vlitos; p. 8: Hulton Deutsch; pp. 14 (top), 16, 23: Panos Pictures; p. 19: Palestine Liberation Organization; p. 21 (top right): Alan Bennett; p. 28: Frank Spooner Pictures.